SECRETS OF THE DEAD

JOHN TOWNSEND

WOW! facts

NOT FOR THE SQUEAMISH!

Badger Publishing Limited
Oldmedow Road,
Hardwick Industrial Estate,
King's Lynn PE30 4JJ
Telephone: 01438 791037

www.badgerlearning.co.uk

2 4 6 8 10 9 7 5 3

Secrets of the Dead ISBN 978-1-78147-579-9

Publisher: Susan Ross
Senior Editor: Danny Pearson
Designer: Fiona Grant

Photos: Cover image: REX/Design Pics Inc
Page 4: Marco Di Lauro/Stringer/Getty Images
Page 5: Andrzej Grygiel/epa/Corbis
Page 6: Jim West/Alamy
Page 8: Niall Carson/PA Archive/Press Association Images
Page 9: Richard Ashworth/Robert Harding Picture Library Ltd/Alamy
Page 10: Paul Hanny/Gamma-Rapho via Getty Images
Page 11: AFP/Getty Images
Page 12: Demetrio Carrasco/Dorling Kindersley/Getty Images
Page 13: Maria Stenzel/National Geographic/Getty Images
Page 15: WitR/iStock/Thinkstock by Getty Images
Page 16: Sipa Press/REX
Page 17: Isifa Image Service sro/REX
Page 18: Kenneth Garrett/National Geographic/Getty Images
Page 20: G. Dagli Orti/De Agostini/Getty Images
Page 23: O. Louis Mazzatenta/National Geographic/Getty Images
Page 25: King Richard III/Alamy
Page 26: Rui Vieira/PA Wire/Press Association Images
Page 28: Andrzej Grygiel/epa/Corbis

Attempts to contact all copyright holders have been made.
If any omitted would care to contact Badger Learning, we will be happy to make appropriate arrangements.

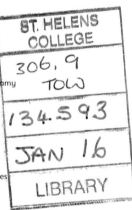

Contents

1. BONE DETECTIVES

'Dead men tell no tales' – so they say. Wrong!

Dead bodies and bones can say a lot. They can often tell scientists about secrets from hundreds of years ago. Like CSI teams who find clues from crime scenes, scientists called 'forensic anthropologists' study human remains to find out about the past. Sometimes what they find is truly amazing.

You might be surprised at what else human bones can tell an expert. They can sometimes solve mysteries from thousands of years ago.

Newspapers report stories like this all the time:

SKELETONS FOUND!

Workmen laying new water pipes have made a grisly discovery. They dug up the remains of four human bodies.

It was a scary sight, which caused much panic. When experts arrived on the scene, they found out the skeletons were from Roman times and had been buried for hundreds of years.

The forensic experts began to study the site, which had not been disturbed since 400 AD. They discovered the bones were of three adults and a child.

There were also two urns containing human ashes.

A 'bone detective' needs to answer many questions about a mystery skeleton:
- How old is it?
- How did the person die?
- Who was it?

The last question might seem impossible to answer when the bones are really old. Even so, science can sometimes reveal more than you might think.

Special tests in a science lab can show how old a bone is. It is also possible to work out from the joints, bones and teeth how old the person was. The smoother the skull, the older the person was likely to be. The age of a child can be worked out from the development of the bones of the wrist.

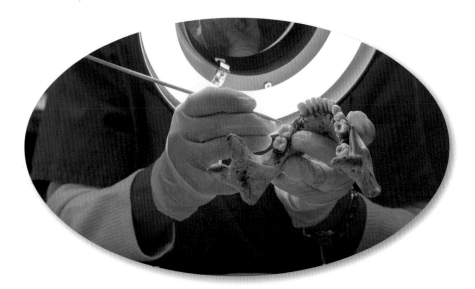

The shape of the pelvis, skull and jaw bone will show if the person was male or female. By measuring the length of the leg and arm bones, experts can work out how tall the person was. Other clues will tell how heavy the person was and possibly their race.

Apart from giving clues about the person's size and health, bones can show how they died. Detectives look for stab marks, skull injuries, broken bones or bullet marks. A damaged throat bone can show if the person was strangled.

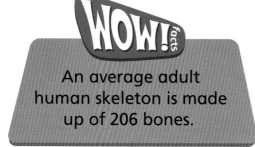

WOW! facts

An average adult human skeleton is made up of 206 bones.

2. FLESH AND BONES

Many clues about the past can be found in human remains buried in bogs, ice or snow. Frozen bodies or those 'pickled' in peat can still have skin, hair, tissue and organs. Their cells can give scientists all kinds of information.

In 2011, the body of a man was found in an Irish bog. He had been there for 4,000 years. Known as Cashel Man, his remains are being studied to find out about life in the Bronze Age.

The body of a man from 2,400 years ago was found in a bog in Denmark. His eyes and mouth were shut and he wore a leather cap. Scientists studied the Tollund Man's preserved body and discovered:

- He was 30 to 40 years old when he died.
- His hair was only 1-2 centimetres long and coloured red by the bog water.
- The cause of death? He had been hanged with a rope.

The ice man

Hikers in the Alps of Austria made a gruesome discovery in 1991 when they came across a frozen body. Scientists got to work and discovered the ice man (they called him Otzi) had been dead for 5,300 years!

It was a mystery as to how Otzi had died. The experts thought he must have died from the cold in the middle of winter. When they looked inside his stomach they found tree pollen, which meant he must have died in summer.

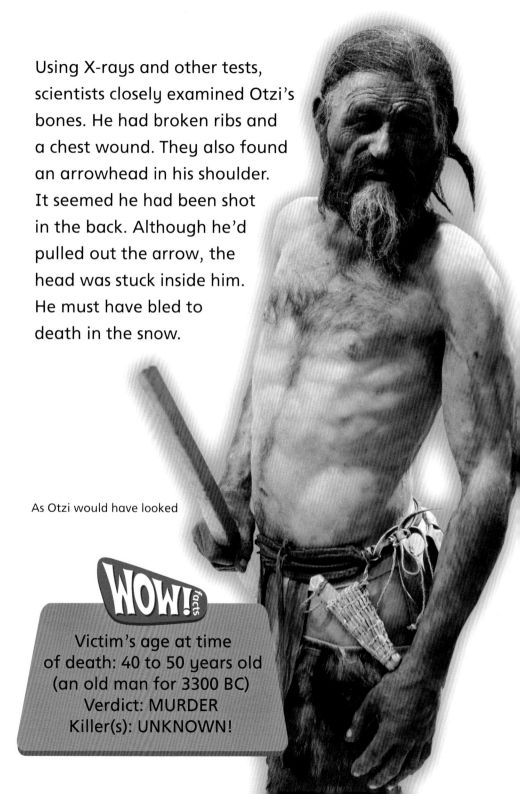

Using X-rays and other tests, scientists closely examined Otzi's bones. He had broken ribs and a chest wound. They also found an arrowhead in his shoulder. It seemed he had been shot in the back. Although he'd pulled out the arrow, the head was stuck inside him. He must have bled to death in the snow.

As Otzi would have looked

WOW! facts

Victim's age at time of death: 40 to 50 years old (an old man for 3300 BC)
Verdict: MURDER
Killer(s): UNKNOWN!

The ice maiden

A frozen female mummy was found in the Andes mountains of Peru in 1995. A volcano had melted the ice and uncovered her body. Scientists began to study 'the ice maiden', who they called Juanita. She had died about 500 years ago.

By using modern forensic tests, scientists found some of Juanita's secrets:

- Her body showed no signs of broken bones or disease.
- She was slim and had eaten meat and vegetables just before her death.
- Her bones, teeth and muscles showed her to be a healthy girl of 12-14 years of age.

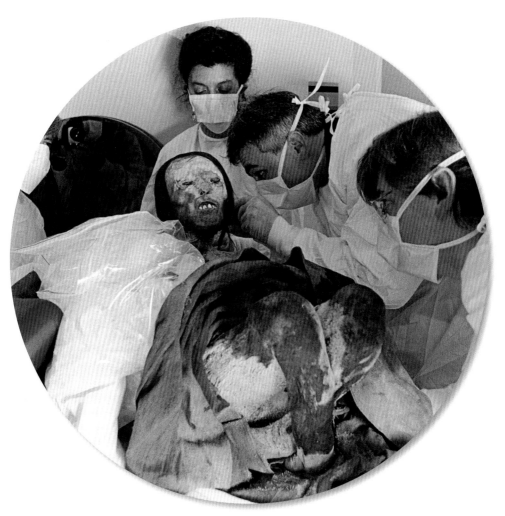

Scientists examining Juanita, the ice maiden

Juanita's skull was damaged above her right eye. A brain injury had caused her death. She had probably been hit on the head with a club and killed as a sacrifice to please the Inca gods.

2 SECRETS IN THE PYRAMIDS

The pyramids of Egypt were built about 4,500 years ago as giant tombs for Egypt's royal families (pharaohs). The Egyptians believed their dead leaders had to be mummified to preserve them.

Forensic scientists have worked out the 'mummy recipe':

- Wash the body.
- Remove all the organs from inside the body – apart from the heart. That will be needed in the afterlife.
- Push a long hook up the nose to mash up the brain, and pull it out through the nostrils.
- Stuff the body with a type of salt called natron. This dries out all the insides and stops them rotting.
- Cover the whole body with natron.
- After 40 days or so, take out all the stuffing and replace with cloth or sawdust.
- Cover the skin in oils.
- Wrap the whole body in strips of cloth and cover in a sheet.
- Put the body in a stone coffin called a sarcophagus. Seal it tightly.
- The mummy will now last forever and is ready for the afterlife.

Sealed inside the pyramids with their treasures, dead pharaohs were ready to become gods in the next world.

Forensic scientists have put mummies in scanners and gathered a lot of data. Experts have been able to make accurate models of some of the pharaohs' faces. A few secrets have been revealed… as you will now discover.

Tutankhamen

The English archaeologist Howard Carter discovered a tomb in Egypt's 'Valley of the Kings' in 1922. Hidden inside was the mummy of the boy-king Tutankhamen.

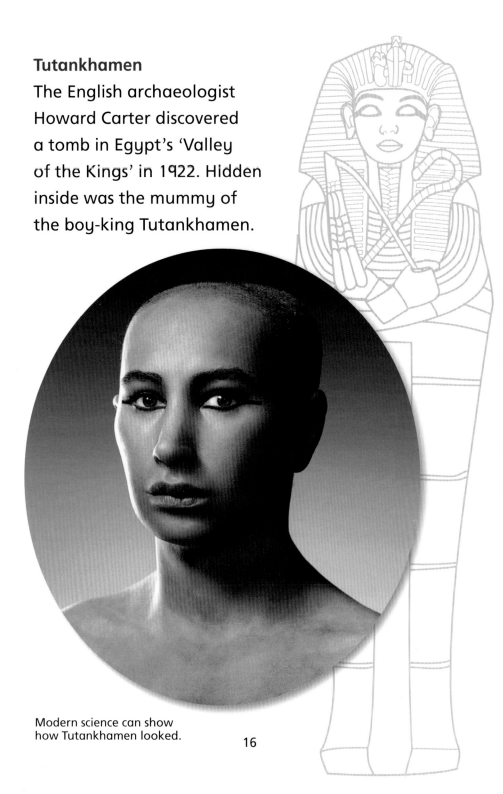

Modern science can show how Tutankhamen looked.

The small tomb was full of treasures, including a golden death mask. It is only in recent years that modern forensic science has revealed secrets about the boy-king from 3,300 years ago. We now know this powerful leader was in fact sick, lame and in pain for much of his short life.

Tutankhamen became pharaoh at the age of about ten in 1333BC and ruled for nine years. For many years, historians wondered why he died so young. A hole in his skull led many to think he had been murdered. Experts now think the hole was made when he was being mummified – by the hook used to remove his brain.

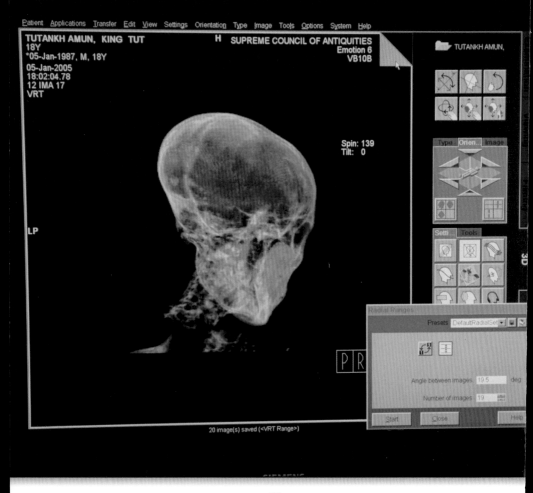

DNA tests and CT scans on Tutankhamen's remains show he had a club foot and weak bones. He probably had to walk with sticks.

The secret of his death was thought to be a bite from a mosquito. Then, in 2013, British experts used a special microscope to scan the mummy.

They discovered the body hadn't been mummified properly so it 'cooked and burned' inside the coffin.

It now seems as if the young king was killed by a chariot crashing into him – shattering his ribs and pelvis and crushing his heart.

The plot thickens!

Some people believe that the pyramids found in Egypt were built by aliens. A few of the pyramids even line up exactly with the stars in the night sky. Strange images of alien-type creatures appear on the inside walls of pyramids. Egyptian writing tells about the sky opening and lights shining down on them. Could these lights have been alien spaceships?

4. VOLCANO SECRETS

For over 250 years, secrets have been dug up from the volcanic ash around Mount Vesuvius in Italy. The secret life of the city of Pompeii was buried and forgotten in 79 AD for over 1,600 years.

Then, in 1748, a few remains of houses and objects were unearthed. Next came the grisly remains of hundreds of people. It was as if they had been frozen in time since being buried under metres of debris from the eruption of Vesuvius. Most victims died instantly as the scorching air burned their lungs, cooked their flesh and melted their brains. Their bodies were buried in ash and preserved for hundreds of years.

Did you know?

- The nearby city of Herculaneum was also destroyed.
- Archaeologists found holes in the ashes that were once the bodies of people that were buried. By pouring plaster into these holes, scientists have been able to make detailed casts of many of the citizens of Pompeii.
- The 'plaster mummies' reveal the human tragedy of Pompeii and life in Roman times.

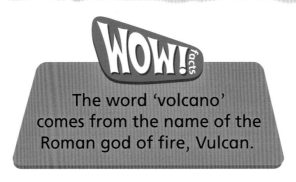

WOW! facts

The word 'volcano' comes from the name of the Roman god of fire, Vulcan.

Pompeii and Herculaneum

Fifteen thousand people in Pompeii and around five thousand in Herculaneum were going about their daily lives when disaster struck. Some objects were preserved that show what people were doing at the time. One victim was clutching a wooden box filled with surgical tools – maybe he was a doctor on his way to save those already injured.

At Herculaneum, all that remained of the victims were their skeletons. The fierce heat there instantly destroyed most things. Work on the skeletons has given scientists information about the people's height, health and even what type of work they did.

One secret to emerge from the bones was that many Romans had a high level of lead in their bodies. Many must have suffered from lead poisoning. This would have affected their minds. The lead got into the water supply from lead pipes, as well as into wine from lead pots used for boiling grapes. Wine really did go to their heads!

5. ROYAL SECRETS

When kings, queens and rulers died long ago, their remains were sometimes lost during wars. That could lead to all kinds of stories and mysteries. Now and again, modern bone detectives can shed light on some of those royal secrets.

The Wars of the Roses were a series of battles between the House of York and the House of Lancaster for the throne of England (1450s to the 1480s). The wars ended when Henry Tudor (House of Lancaster and later King Henry VII) defeated King Richard III (House of York).

Richard, the last Yorkist king of England, was killed at the Battle of Bosworth Field in 1485. He was quickly buried in a church – which was later pulled down.

The white rose of York and the red rose of Lancaster

24

Richard III died and was buried in Leicestershire.

Many stories grew about Richard. William Shakespeare added to them when he wrote a play that showed Richard as an evil hunchback with a shrivelled arm. He was accused by many of murdering his nephews – the 'Princes in the Tower' – who disappeared in 1483. There is no evidence that he was responsible and their fate remains a mystery to this day. So did the fate of Richard III's grave... until the bulldozers arrived...

The king in the car park

In 2012, archaeologists began to dig up a car park in Leicester. They hoped to find King Richard's final resting place. Suddenly they uncovered a skeleton. Forensic scientists rushed to the scene. Could it really be the long-lost king from 527 years before?

Sure enough, the skeleton did have a curved spine and was a man from the exact period of King Richard III. Scientists tested DNA from the bones with a living descendant of the king. Guess what – it was a perfect match! Tests proved this was Richard's skeleton.

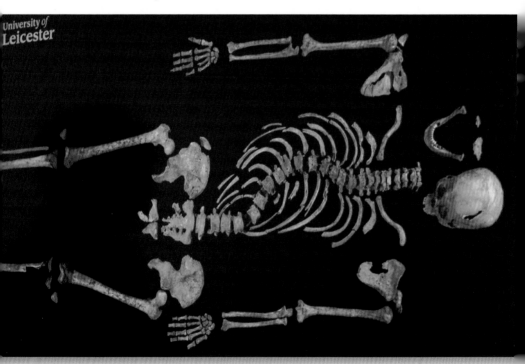

University of Leicester

Further work on King Richard's skeleton revealed a number of secrets:

- Richard III was killed by two blows to his skull – on the battlefield. One strike appeared to have 'sliced away' part of the skull, and the other would have stabbed his brain.
- The dead king had been stabbed in the behind. It seemed his body had been stripped, tied at the hands and dragged by a horse, before being stabbed and quickly buried.
- Scientists found further wounds to the king's ribs and pelvis. Even though the king was hunchbacked, he did not have a shrivelled arm. Shakespeare had been wrong!

King Richard died at the age of 32 after one of the shortest reigns ever – only 26 months as king.

6. VAMPIRES AND PLAGUES

Hundreds of years ago, many people believed in the 'undead' or vampires. They did not realise that dead bodies could move and make noises when they start to rot. Gases inside a corpse's stomach can gurgle, and the fingernails and hair still appear to grow. In fact, it's just that the skin is shrinking. People often feared the dead were coming alive again!

During the Middle Ages, the fear of vampires was very real. To protect themselves from the undead, people often buried bodies in special ways. (If you are squeamish, look away now!)

When workers building a road in Poland dug up four skeletons, they were amazed the skulls had been buried between the legs. Why?

Scientists dated the bones as 500-600 years old. That was a time when anyone thought to be a vampire was beheaded. Another punishment was to be hanged and left until the neck rotted so the head fell off. People believed that a vampire would not be able to rise from the grave if it couldn't find its head!

Skeletons have been found in Bulgaria with iron rods through them and their teeth missing. The iron rods were to pin dead bodies into their graves to stop them from getting out.

Voices from the grave

In 2013, a mass grave was discovered in London by workers building a new railway line. The human remains were in an ancient burial ground that had been used in the 14th century for victims of the 'Black Death' plague. This site was called 'No Man's Land' and contained the bodies of up to 50,000 victims of the epidemic of the 1350s. Since 1500, its whereabouts had been lost...

The skeletons they found were in two neat rows. This area must have been used at the start of the plague when death rates were low. Later, hundreds of bodies were buried together to save space.

Scientists hope to study DNA from the teeth of the victims and even find DNA of the plague bacteria. Who knows what secrets they might find?

The Black Death was carried in fleas that lived on rats' bodies. If a person was unfortunate enough to receive an infected flea bite, they would probably be dead within 2-4 days.

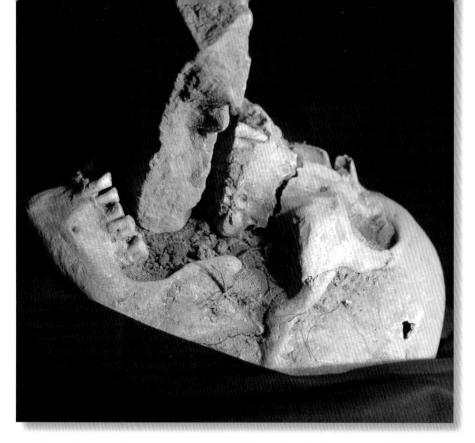

Italy also suffered plagues. The Black Death killed over 50,000 people in Venice in 1576. In a mass grave from that time, historians recently found a puzzling skeleton. It was a woman with a brick wedged between her teeth. It seems people believed vampires were spreading the plague. Bricks were placed in the mouths of likely vampires to stop them from biting anyone and spreading the disease. Just another secret of the dead.

Sweet dreams!

INDEX